Presented to

____

____

By

____

____

~ OMAR STUENKEL

Marriage Is for Two

How to Build a Marriage That Lasts and Works

AUGSBURG Publishing House • Minneapolis

MARRIAGE IS FOR TWO

Contents

Preface

Marriage is a good thing. It is possible to say that on the testimony of countless human beings who have experienced it. It is also true because at creation God made man and woman to live as husband and wife, complementing each other.

The love a man and woman share in marriage makes it the closest human relationship. Marriage is exciting, satisfying, and fulfilling when the love between husband and wife is mutual, when it is faithful and dependable, and when it rests not only on feeling but also on will. For though one may have felt love for many, in marriage each chooses the other as husband and wife permanently and sees him or her as a gift of God.

How marriage comes about, that is, how a man and woman come to be recognized as husband and wife depends more on the society in which they live than on the direction of God. All that is implied in the Bible is some form of mutual acceptance and a commitment to one another as husband and wife.

From the words of Jesus and other statements in the Bible, it is evident that the commitment and the marriage bond ideally are to be lifelong. But even the words of Jesus, reported in Matthew 19, indicate that the marriage may be terminated, while both partners are alive, if one proves completely unfaithful. Paul the Apostle also indicates to the Corinthians that there are circumstances when one must accept the dissolution of a marriage. Either death or divorce may separate husband and wife. These are tragic realities, of course, but they face life as it really is.

Since marriage is the closest of all human relationships and potentially the most rewarding, it deserves the best human effort. A good marriage is evidence of the grace of God who gives us in so many ways what we do not merit. A good marriage, one that is wholesome and happy for the couple and a blessing to others, does not happen without effort: God joins people in marriage by how they treat one another for the rest of their lives. Marriage, in that sense, is a process rather than an event.

To say that marriage is for two emphasizes the mutuality of the relationship. One partner may be faithful, tender, and good, but if the other is careless or callous about the marriage, the relationship will struggle, falter, or fail. In a good relationship the benefits of marriage are mutual; the responsibilities should also be shared.

I learned much in the 32 years of my own marriage to a good, loving, loyal, and beautiful woman until she joined the Lord in death. I have learned much, too, from the experiences and observations of others, not only in many counseling sessions, but from books, sem-

8

inars, and workshops on marriage. More recently I have gained new and different insights through a second marriage to another good and thoughtful wife.

What I offer here is drawn from all these experiences as a husband, student, counselor, and pastor for more than 30 years. What I have written is based on the ideas I explore with young couples who come to be married. It is my hope that parents of such couples, as well as the couples themselves, will read these pages. I believe, too, that many who have been married a while can benefit from what is stated here. Likewise, it is my hope that pastors and other marriage counselors will use this book to guide couples to a better marriage.

It is my firm conviction that a good marriage is one of life's choicest blessings for which we should pray God and for which we should often thank him.

One

Celebrate Your Wedding

Have fun as you plan your wedding. Some tensions are inevitable, but too easily wedding planning becomes grim and complicated. It's good to have as big a wedding and as extensive a reception as you can afford—but not more.

Big weddings are wise because, if properly planned, they become memorable events for the entire family. They unite relatives around a happy occasion, and they furnish the couple with the recognition of a change in life and status that is psychologically beneficial. Human beings need to dramatize rites of passage to make them real.

Above all, weddings in church are celebrations of the goodness of God. Life on earth is not all a vale of tears. Into our frail and faulty human condition, God allows his mercy to show in something as sublime as a marriage of love. To find someone whom you can trust for life, whether circumstances get better or worse, is a great blessing, but to cement that relationship with the kind of love found only in marriage calls for exuberant celebration.

IF PROBLEMS ARISE

Sometimes, of course, problems rise early that signal life will not be a bowl of cherries. Since marriage is for two, adjustments and negotiations are necessary.

Mike and Laurel had found a hall that could accommodate their wedding reception four months later; a local printer promised to have their invitations ready in three weeks; and they had met with the clergyman who was to marry them. But then things started to go wrong.

Both the best man and the maid of honor they chose had already committed themselves for other plans on the date of the wedding. Laurel's father had insisted that at least 15 of his close associates at work be invited, and that opened up the problem as to whether Mike's father would include the dozen employees in his small business. But the crowning problem turned out to be Aunt Susie. She had sung at Laurel's mother's wedding and let it be known that she expected to do the same for Laurel.

As subtle tensions mounted and Mike kept saying the decisions were up to Laurel, the couple began to discover that being together didn't seem as much fun as it had been. There were too many complicated decisions, and it seemed that other people were crowding into their personal relationship.

They wondered whether all this hassle was necessary. They just wanted to get married. Why couldn't they simply have their blood tests, get a marriage license, go to a minister, and be married? It would accomplish the same purpose, save a lot of money, and eliminate all the hassle.

When they talked about it seriously—especially after discovering the price of wedding gowns—both Mike and Laurel tried to make it sound as though the simplest ceremony and celebration possible was what they really wanted. But then they found that much of the excitement and fun had gone out of things, and even their relationship to one another seemed strained and artificial.

When she was alone, Laurel cried. She wondered why things had to get so complicated. It had all seemed so wonderful and exciting when she and Mike first talked about the wedding.

What should they do? By talking about their problems with their pastor, they came to see better how to share and shape decisions, when to yield to others in their plans and when to stand firm together.

Planning a wedding is good preparation for being married. It is a "for real" test of communication, cooperation, understanding, and relationship. Many of the pressures and tensions of planning a wedding are the same as occur in marriage. There are decisions to be made—and a groom who leaves all decisions in the hands of the bride is off to a shaky start. After all, marriage is for two.

There is also the sensitive matter of the money needed —and this test of relationship strains both the lines of communication and the sense of judgment. There are human relationships as well as relatives to recognize— and to please one sometimes means to displease another.

A general principle Mike and Laurel might have found useful is that it is worthwhile having the biggest wedding celebration you can afford, but it is not worthwhile to have a bigger one than you can afford. That principle has a corollary: bride and groom should make decisions together and announce them. They should listen to advice, but the decisions and the consequences are theirs.

RITUAL CAN BE USEFUL

Formal church weddings and gala receptions are important for the bride and groom because human beings need to ritualize major moments of their lives. Marriage is the most significant voluntary change in the human situation; it needs to be ritualized.

Ritual is a means of establishing the significance of what is happening by words and actions to signify specific commitments. Rituals help us accept who we are and what we may expect in relationships with other people. According to its significance, a ritual may be as simple as a handshake or as elaborate as a presidential inauguration. It may mark a funeral, baptism, or confirmation, but it also accompanies secular events like the opening of an important bridge or the welcoming of returning heroes.

Ritual events often include festive or commemorative eating or drinking together. The more significant the bond established or celebrated, the more elaborate is the festive meal likely to be.

If significant ritual and communal celebration occur, the newly married bride and groom are more able to realize and express their new status as husband and wife. Relatives, too, find it easier to accept and support them in this new role.

A wedding is a joyous time. Few occasions in life

open as many new important possibilities or promise as much personal satisfaction. Furthermore, the choice the couple has made is voluntary and considered. Good feelings run high and promise great mutual happiness. Love rules.

A wedding is joyous, therefore, in part because a man and a woman have freely, without compulsion or control, chosen one another. On the wedding day the choice seems so promising, so fortunate, so mutually loving, that the couple is ecstatic—and the guests reflect that joy.

CHURCH WEDDINGS

Let's look at what happens in a church wedding service.

First of all, it is a worship service; therefore, the setting, the music, and the conduct of all participants should show reverence and thoughtfulness. The wedding worship, like all worship services, seeks to glorify God, to witness to his merciful presence and power, and to call for commitment from people.

A Christian wedding should normally take place in that building, the church, which a group of believers have set aside for hearing God's Word and offering their prayers. For important reasons, however, a Christian wedding may be held in a home or at some other appropriate place.

When you announce your desire to be husband and wife in your wedding invitations, you call together those who mean most to you as family and friends. You ask them to assemble that they may share with you in a public occasion of the greatest importance to you. The occasion is the open and binding commitment, to which you have already privately agreed, to be husband and wife. From society's perspective the ceremony establishes you as husband and wife. In more personal terms, the two of you have now become one.

The marriage ceremony provides a generally accepted framework for making public and legal a covenant of trust and loyalty already privately agreed upon. By the ceremony the community ratifies and consents to the couple's choice. Because a marriage ceremony represents more than a private agreement, couples who plan their own marriage ritual tend to be far less radical in the phrases they select than they had originally planned. Probably for this reason some couples who start out to construct their own ritual soon abandon the attempt in favor of a traditional rite, with a prayer or some personal selection added to make it more directly their own.

In the common marriage ritual great emphasis is laid on demonstrating that the choice of both bride and groom is voluntary and carefully considered. It is as though the minister were saying, "Now of all the persons you may have loved, could love, or will love, do you truly choose *this* person to be from this day on your husband or wife?"

To clarify and emphasize what is happening, most rituals seek four separate assents. First is the assent expressed by "I do" or "I will." Next, both man and woman repeat the vows. Then, as an enduring sign of commitment other than words, rings are exchanged. Finally, there is the sign of mutual agreement in our society, the clasping of the right hands. Consent and commitment have been established publicly and before God.

By publicly announcing your desire to be husband and wife, you make it more believable to yourselves and more apparent to others that you really are permanently linked in life and destiny. What happens to one will not only affect the other, but will also be of primary concern to the other.

The instruction, read as part of the service or given as a sermon, also reenforces the responsibilities and blessings of marriage. Such instruction is useful not only for the wedding couple, but also to remind guests of the meaning of marital commitment.

THINGS TO CONSIDER

1. How can the bride and groom establish their new independence from parental control and still show respect, receive counsel, and give love?
2. Is it right for the groom to leave most decisions and plans for the wedding to the bride?
3. How is preparation for the wedding a "for real" test of the pressures of being married?
4. What are some important elements of the ritual of a wedding?
5. What are some of the components of joy at a wedding?
6. What are the advantages of a church wedding?
7. What besides consent is essential for a marriage?

Two

Seek Companionship
and Friendship

Companionship and friendship are two of the most enduring aspects of a good marriage. To enjoy being together, whether others are present or not, is a test of marital compatibility. If you look forward to the other's coming and feel secure in each other's love when you are apart, you have companionship and friendship. Unless treasured and cultivated, however, both can be lost.

Phil liked to play softball, and was good at it. In addition, he was an organizer. So after he married Amy, he not only played softball twice a week, he also coached a team.

Though Amy was proud of Phil's prowess and popularity, by the second year of marriage she began to feel dissatisfied with so much attention to sports. It was then she discovered a trait in Phil she hadn't realized before: Phil needed the approval softball gave him so much that he preferred it to the responsibilities of establishing a home. For him marriage was for two—but only so one could have its advantages, while the other took almost all the responsibilities.

When Amy suggested he give less time to the sport, Phil replied that she should be glad he wasn't spending his time drinking or running after other women. So Amy let it go, tried to enjoy going to ball games, and took up crafts to occupy her time when Phil was gone. But trouble was brewing.

COMPLEX COMPANIONSHIP

Their relationship suggests a number of common but complex problems in marriage. Many men live out the compulsions pictured in John Updike's *Run, Rabbit, Run* or by Biff in Arthur Miller's *Death of a Salesman*. For them the center spotlight they experienced in high school or college sports remains the uneasy goal of their adult life. Relationships built on mature acceptance of their own limitations, coupled with loyal companionship in marriage, seem unnecessary or unsatisfying to them.

Some husbands think it is enough for them to be good providers and bed partners. Only reluctantly, if at all, do they assume equal responsibility for the couple's intellectual or social life. Church and school are left to the wife, or the husband lets it be evident that he participates only to please her.

For any participation in the full goals of a marriage relationship such a male expects gratitude and appreciation. He feels abused if his wife seems to complain. After all, he says, he does more than some men do, and he isn't carousing around.

Phil and Amy needed a common focus outside of

their personal relationship to give added meaning to their lives. If both Phil and Amy could direct some energy toward helping others in a way both found meaningful, their communication would improve and their sense of adult responsibility would mature. In marriage you need a focus outside the marriage itself which is significant to both. It must be a mutual interest.

Marriage is for companionship more than anything else. Husband and wife should like being together. It is important that they be friends as well as lovers. Marital friendship goes far beyond "His and Hers" towels or look-alike ski sweaters. It is the kind of mutual contentment in one another's company envisaged in the original creation. When it was found that of all the animals and birds God created and Adam named "not one of them was a suitable companion to help him," God created the woman Eve. Then comes the succinct observation: "That is why a man leaves his father and mother and is united with his wife, and they become one" (Gen. 2:24). Of all human relationships, the bond between husband and wife is to be the dearest, exceeding even the closest ties of blood.

Sometimes couples did not think too much about companionship when they decided to marry. Physical attraction or the need to escape a bad home life may have been uppermost in their minds. Newly married couples can help one another talk about their feelings and develop mutual expectations for growing companionship.

Essential as it is, the bond of companionship and friendship between husband and wife should not become a jealous possessiveness which will not tolerate friendships outside the marriage. Nor should companionship imply that a couple must do everything together.

Each also remains an individual with a need for privacy, with interests which may be different from the partner's, and with independent decisions, friendships, and habits. In that way, marriage is for two who remain two and are not blended into one.

INDIVIDUALITY VS. DEPENDENCE

Although women have asserted their individuality more than before, it still happens that young wives show an excessive dependence on their mothers. A young husband may complain, "My wife is always on the phone talking to her mother." Often this daughter-mother relationship has serious consequences for the marriage.

Not only are the couple's times together strained by the wife's long conversations with her mother, but the couple's decisions are often second-guessed because "my mother doesn't think that's a good idea." Frequently a young wife finds it so difficult to move away from the parent's community that her husband must turn down opportunities which beckon him in a distant place.

The other side of this problem is the husband's posture of apology for being married. When his friends want to stop somewhere after work, a man may not dare to say that for him it is important to get home to his wife. Some husbands feel it is weakness in them to do what marriage calls for, that is, to put his wife's needs and desires ahead of those of other human beings. To be dominated by a wife, emotionally or financially, earns a man the fearsome designation "henpecked." There will be times, of course, when acceding to plans of comrades or meeting human needs other than those of wife or husband is perfectly consistent with love of one's spouse—but not when it is done because one is ashamed to be married.

You show companionship and friendship in marriage when you are happy and content just to be together, whatever you may be doing. If you always need other people around or always have to be going somewhere to be happy, your companionship and friendship is not what it should be. On the other hand, neither should a husband spend every night before the television set while his wife fills her time as best she can. That is scarcely a model of marital companionship.

Some couples have interests in gardening, hobbies, or sports like golf, tennis, or fishing that coincide and make their companionship simpler recreationally. Others develop mutual interests in reading, restoring furniture, or playing games with the children. Many Christians find a common bond of interest and service to their congregation. But for some, work schedules that seldom coincide, responsibilities of their jobs that are excessive, poor health, or out-of-town travel make being together very difficult.

Some people love activity; others prefer quiet and serenity. Some are stay-at-homes; others love travel, cruises, or dining out. If you just pursue individual preferences without bending to the needs or desires of the partner, the result will be a marriage in name only or divorce. You are allowed such differences if you show consideration for the other in a way that holds companionship and friendship as high priorities.

Instead of supporting one another and drawing on the strength of one another, some marry simply as a convenience. It is, after all, very convenient to be married. To have someone with whom to eat, sleep, and go out socially makes one more acceptable for our society and generally offers advantages beyond reduced cost for car insurance. Marriage also makes it easier to maintain a house, to care for a lawn, to get one's groceries, and to pay the rent. Don't let your marriage become simply a convenience.

TWO JOBS OR ONE?

It is so common for both spouses to be employed outside the home that it may happen during at least part of your marriage too. The decision to opt for two jobs should be made carefully. Some couples think they need two incomes to maintain a certain standard of living. The first question when considering income, therefore, is, what minimum standard of living do you consider desirable?

But money is not the only consideration. Both husband and wife may feel that self-fulfillment and meaning cannot be achieved without careers—though for some kinds of employment "career" seems a rather pretentious title. Possibly greater satisfaction and fulfillment could be achieved either by volunteer service in church or community or by developing productive skills at home.

Sometimes a wife may desire employment outside the home just for the sake of "getting out" more regularly. A job has sometimes helped persons who otherwise felt confined. Where part-time employment is available, the pressure may be relieved by less than full-time work.

If both of you work outside the home, there are realistic problems to consider. Meals, clothing, cars, vacations, children, church responsibilities and other areas

24

of life are affected. When you have young children, the problem is vastly increased.

The basic questions are the standard of living and the style of life which promise most meaning, usefulness, and satisfaction for you. The constant measure of the value of your life is this: how do we best honor God and care about people in a way that gives meaning, purpose, and joy to our lives?

THINGS TO CONSIDER

1. How much time away from their "companionship" in marriage is wise and good for husband and wife?
2. What does the statement "marriage is for companionship more than anything else" mean to you?
3. What degree of jealousy is acceptable in marriage?
4. How definite is the obligation of husbands and wives toward one another in the perspective of "not owning" one another?
5. Discuss: "Marriage is not bondage to a letter of the law but the free and ready sacrifice of selfishness or convenience for the sake of love."
6. What is a "marriage of convenience"?
7. Does an acceptable standard of living require a dual income?
8. What is a constant measure of the value of a lifestyle?

Three

Trust Is the Key

Have you seen older couples exchange merry, understanding glances that seemed to speak warmth and affection? When such an exchange happens, you can be sure they have attained a high level of trust.

Trust can be conveyed by spoken messages or in unspoken ways. It can be violated by the same means. Because it is emotional as well as logical, trust needs special nurture. Tell one another what you like and appreciate about the other, but show by your actions that your words are not hollow.

Deep trust takes time to develop. As you live together through experiences of all kinds and see that the other is firm in concern for you and dependable in relationship, trust will grow. There will be times of testing too.

Whenever David came home a little later than Laura expected, she would greet him with the words, "Where have you been?'' The way she said it always had the ring of accusation. To David it sounded as though Laura was saying, ''What have you been doing that is illicit, immoral, or irresponsible?''

That wasn't what Laura usually intended. It was just that she counted so on David coming home. But it was true, sometimes she did wonder whether he delayed because he would rather not come home. It made her jealous and defensive.

As this was repeated, tension developed, so that eventually David just replied with a meaningless grunt or said bluntly, ''I come home when I want to.'' This worried Laura even more.

Not until they went to seek counsel from their pastor did they realize what was happening. A vicious circle had developed. What was at first simply Laura's fear was slowly becoming reality: David was postponing coming home because he dreaded the daily confrontation that seemed like an inquisition.

When the pastor by careful questions helped them see that they still sincerely wanted to be husband and wife and that they desired this strain of suspicion to be eliminated, they realized how a simple misunderstanding can build to a marriage crisis.

The question, ''Where have you been?'' is not out of place in marriage. Used sincerely and with appropriate tone of voice, it can reflect the normal and proper concern of one spouse for the other which the close relationship of marriage assumes. Ordinarily the question should be answered, simply, directly, and without hostility. If that is done, it will not become a source of tension.

Should the question appear to come too frequently or unnecessarily, then the spouse who feels that way should quietly explain to the other that irritation is beginning to rise. Any husband or wife can easily slip into patterns which bother the other because they convey undue and unnecessary concern or control over the other's individuality. The balance between loving care and oversolicitous control is not easily struck.

TRUST GROWS

What is at stake in the experience just related is the core of a marriage relationship, namely, trust. Trust in marriage does not only mean that neither spouse need fear that the other is being unfaithful. Trust in marriage means the constant confidence that the other is *for* you, not against you. Even when one spouse is foolish, stubborn, or difficult, the other can be secure in the confidence that nothing malicious, unfeeling, or vengeful is intended.

That kind of trust gives stability, strength, and serenity to a marriage. Each feels sure that at least one person in the whole universe is loyal and true to what he or she sees as best for the other. Knowing that someone will seek your good whatever comes and stand by even when he or she believes you foolish, wrong, or impulsive, gives strength and peace that can come in no other way. This does not mean that husband and wife always approve of one another's attitudes or actions or even condone them, but they care for one another and show it nevertheless.

Such love and trust between husband and wife should be the primary characteristic of a mature marital relationship. But young couples, early in marriage, should not despair or even be surprised if they have not yet attained such trust. It takes experiences of all kinds, sad and beautiful, trivial and profound, in which doubts and fears about the other's loyalty have been overcome by perceiving that though the other may not always be wise or thoughtful, still there was the desire to stand together in mutual support. God's plan to make man and woman companions and helpers of one another in marriage can be fulfilled.

Trust must underlie everything so that you can assume that your spouse always intends to do only what is best for you. Human frailty, of course, intrudes even into this noblest relationship and allows not only weaknesses but also willfulness to make forgiveness of one another necessary.

The words of Paul to the Ephesians might well be applied to marriage: "Get rid of all bitterness, passion, and anger. No more shouting or insults, no more hateful feelings of any sort. Instead, be kind and tenderhearted to one another, and forgive one another, as God has forgiven you through Christ." In that spirit it needs to be said that striking one's wife, for whatever reason, should be unconditionally taboo. Nothing is gained by it, and the damage done to trust by this tragic action is never completely erased.

SACRIFICIAL LOVE

The love and trust for which couples are to strive in marriage must include a willingness to sacrifice oneself for the sake of the other. In Ephesians 5:21-33 we have a thought-provoking description of the love and trust relationship between husband and wife in terms of self-sacrifice. Married couples would do well to read and meditate on these words of Paul again and again.

In the routine of daily life sacrificial love in marriage

means that no partner can make personal plans or reach personal decisions without thinking: how will this affect my spouse? Just as no one puts a member of his body in pain or jeopardy for the benefit of another part without serious consideration, so one partner in a marriage always considers the consequences of his or her actions for the other. This is also why communication in marriage is so important.

It is good to look for signals in marriage that spell trouble or success. If you suddenly realize that you feel day after day that your spouse thinks only of himself or herself and not of you, that is a serious danger signal. The feeling may or may not be valid, but you need to recognize and deal with it.

If one or both of the marriage partners persistently feel this way, they are only one step away from serious consideration of divorce. For this sense of neglect creates a feeling of being a nonperson to the other, which the marriage relationship cannot tolerate. Bickering, fighting, and nagging begin to develop, or else such division in spirit takes place that each leads a separate life under the same roof. Sometimes the wife will find with her children the relationship she lacks with her husband, and an unhealthy dependency results.

Whenever either partner continues to feel that the other does not care about his or her desires or feelings, you should seek counseling from a pastor or a marriage counselor, not from relatives, neighbors, or friends. The situation is too complex for simple solutions.

THE VALUE OF COUNSELING

Many couples whose marriages were relatively good, but could be better, have found help in various marriage retreats. Before entering upon such a venture, however, it is important to know who will be leading it and what process will be followed. Not everyone is able to respond to some procedures of self-revelation used in some marriage retreats. Generally, however, church-related marriage retreats have proved of immense benefit to basically sound marriages.

A caution, which may also be a consolation, should be expressed about marriage counseling: parents can rarely help their children's marital problems, and children can almost never solve their parent's marriage difficulties. With rare exceptions they should not even try to get directly involved with counsel or arbitration. Instead, relatives should encourage one another to seek professional help and help to make it financially possible or offer transportation or childcare, if needed, so that counseling can take place.

COPING WITH JEALOUSY

An extreme enemy of trust is jealousy. There is a degree of what may be called jealousy which is appropriate in marriage because it is innate in the concept of "cleaving" only to one another until death parts. Each partner should feel that there is a special closeness, a private world between them, which must not be invaded from the outside and which neither partner may squander by treating others outside the marriage with equal familiarity.

Deep jealousy is extremely difficult to cope with, for every concession to its demands seems to the jealous person only to prove guilt. Most people find it intolerable to live with a really jealous person. That kind of jealousy is an emotional flaw which is seldom admitted and therefore cannot be treated as it should be. Sometimes another person whom the jealous one does trust to some extent can help him or her seek treatment. If this does not happen, it will be at best a very unhappy marriage and will more likely lead to dissolution of the marriage, extreme bitterness, or even illness and death.

Since all human beings sin, willfully or in weakness, also in how they treat one another in marriage, forgiveness is essential. What is meant is not a superficial "I'm sorry, please forgive me," but an honest admission of guilt and regret which receives the response of generous and loving forgiveness and full restoration of trust. It is important that both husband and wife belong to a Christian church where they learn to treasure God's gracious forgiveness for the sake of Jesus Christ.

It takes thought and practice for a married couple to trust and to express trust. The marriage ceremony does not provide it ready-made, nor does any protestation of love, however flowery or well-meant, produce the deep trust a mature marriage experiences. There will be times in any marriage—and often in new marriages—when one partner will think that the other is selfish or that the other no longer considers the needs or wishes of the partner. Therefore too much should not be assumed. The inevitable phrase "You should have known" should not become too common. Instead take time to express your feelings, hopes, and attitudes to one another.

If you resolve in your marriage that you are going to cultivate trust, show trust, and value trust, you will have taken a giant step toward happiness. Tender regard for one another's feelings plus the confidence that you can be uninhibited toward each other is a combination that spells trust. As such trust develops you will begin to show a happy style of marriage that is uniquely your own and does not follow exactly the pattern by which other couples express their marital relationship.

To have one person in this whole wide complex world whom you can trust to have your welfare and happiness at heart whatever comes is a remarkable treasure. Marriage offers that opportunity.

THINGS TO CONSIDER

1. Does the question from spouse to spouse "Where have you been?" require a reply?
2. According to Chapter 2, what is the core of the marriage relationship?
3. Should husband and wife always defend and justify one another to others?
4. In marriage, what helps trust grow?
5. To what extent should self-sacrifice go in marriage according to Ephesians 5:21-33?
6. Must each partner in marriage always ask in all personal plans and decisions: how will this affect my spouse?
7. What circumstances in marriage waves a "red flag" most frantically?
8. What should be done when either spouse consistently feels that the other does not care about his or her desires or feelings at all?
9. Why is it so difficult to live with a very jealous person?

Four

Communication Helps

In your marriage much of the fun and much of the strength of your relationship will depend on how well you communicate. In time you will develop little inside jokes, references to incidents you shared that make you chuckle. You will also discover some expressions not to use because, for whatever reason, the other cannot tolerate them. Even your style of conversation—and the time for it—has to be gradually developed. Some persons like to talk late at night; others talk at mealtime. Individual differences must be recognized and adjustments made.

When Tom and Jan came in for counseling about their marriage, the pastor asked, "What do you see as the main cause of tension?"

Jan answered immediately: "He never talks to me." Previously their problems had been specific crises when they sought counsel. Once it was the refusal of Jan to move to another state when Tom was offered a job there. Another time Jan was angry at Tom's jealousy, and he was uptight about her evenings away from home.

Tom raised his eyebrows but said nothing until he was asked, "Do you feel, Tom, that you never talk to Jan?"

"I talk to her," he said. "I'm just not a talkative person, and sometimes there isn't much I want to say. So I listen. Besides, Jan seems to think I'm wrong whenever I say anything, so I shut up. I thought it would be more peaceful that way."

The pastor replied, "Perhaps it would help if we looked at what there is to talk about between married people. I'm going to ask each of you to write down five or six subjects you think husbands and wives should talk about. Then we'll go on from there."

We might say the problem between Tom and Jan was communication, but that problem is often deeper than the failure to verbalize. Often the emotional effect of certain subjects makes communication difficult or even impossible. Or it may be that previous experience in the marriage has caused the husband or wife to sense, as Tom did, that the comments he or she might offer would raise resentment, cause tears, or meet rejection, and therefore communication was stopped deliberately. It can happen, too, that one person in the marriage verbalizes everything and the other is much less talkative.

VERBAL SIGNALS

It is a common complaint of wives that husbands too seldom express gratitude, praise, or even love in words. If a husband rarely voices such sentiments to his wife, the complaint is eminently justified. Much that a wife does deserves just those verbal strokes.

On the other hand, men desire from their wives words of confidence in their good intent, their ability, and their judgment. They also need the expressions of love and appreciation that are so often taken for granted.

Many actions of husbands and wives that would otherwise be misjudged will be understood if you state your feelings, acknowledge your fears, and express your hopes. Early in a marriage particularly, it is important for you to give advance notice of plans to your spouse and to tell one another tentative considerations long before final decisions are reached about even minor matters. That kind of communication builds trust.

Not only husbands but also wives need the caution to interpret their actions and attitudes in words. For otherwise these are easily misunderstood. Especially when a wife's actions or decisions include other people— friends, children, or, especially, parents—interpretation is necessary. Husbands tend to become silently jealous when a wife's actions involve her with others. Interpretations can help.

Any husband will find that a word of thanks or praise about a well-prepared meal is gratefully received, not only on special occasions but on ordinary days. Likewise wives should know that a husband wants his wife's genuine interest in things he does at home or at work. Husbands especially need to know that their wives are satisfied with the job the husband holds and consider it worthwhile.

Neither husband nor wife can afford to make public jokes about one another unless they are sure the other does not consider the joke an insult or a cruel jibe. Don't assume too much. The familiar phrase "She knows I'm only kidding" is often not enough to remove the sting of the put-down joke. Furthermore, what the phrase says is often not true. She doesn't think you are only kidding.

NONVERBAL MESSAGES

Communication occurs also in nonverbal ways, of course. A gentle touch, a special smile, a kiss, or even a way of walking, of lifting one's eyebrows, or of closing a door can be understood or misunderstood. The most negative kind of communication in marriage is nonverbal, namely, when a husband strikes his wife. The communication is so negative, so destructive of trust, that the wife who receives such treatment will never forget it.

Verbal communication between husband and wife should be free and easy but thoughtful. Banter is one characteristic of confidence, love, and understanding between husband and wife, and you may develop your own private jokes and verbal signals that give pleasure between you again and again. But when that light and easy banter changes into joking that communicates hurt, criticism, or hidden anger, it is no longer banter. Unfortunately, husbands and wives often use the presence of friends or relatives to voice criticism of one another by what is spoken as a joke and nervously laughed at but which carries an ill-concealed barb that makes knowledgeable guests uncomfortable. Don't use this negative means to communicate.

What is there to talk about between husband and wife? Some sharing of one another's work experiences and hopes should happen. To fail in this area is to cut off one another from what is often one of the most predominant interests of your life. It is comforting and encouraging, too, when you can review periodic hurts, frustrations, and successes in work with someone who cares. Such review makes it easier to keep going.

Husband and wife will naturally talk about their children. In fact, care must be exercised that this concern—and schedules and meals—does not become the sum total of meaningful conversation. A deliberate attempt on the part of both husband and wife to talk about items of community interest, congregational programs, or national issues is wise and good. When children are very young, such conversations at mealtime are difficult because the children demand attention, but they are still possible to some extent. If the children dominate the conversations of the parents, the time will come when the children are grown and the husband and wife face one another as comparative strangers with little common interest.

Mealtime should be a time for the family to be together at least once each day. Schedules of children as well as parents often make this goal hard to accomplish, but keep it as an important objective. At mealtime there should be conversation in which everyone is entitled to participate, but the conversation should not be dominated always by the children. It is God's plan that parents be authority figures, and they should not hesitate to exercise that responsibility with the kind of love and consideration that prevents them from becoming tyrannical.

Television has changed the pattern of mealtime and of family conversations in the home, just as it has changed so much of our culture generally. That consideration should be recognized and dealt with in the family in a way that takes into account the need for meaningful interpersonal conversation by all members of the family. Again, it is necessary that parents be in control, and that husband and wife both recognize the need for significant communication between them and with other members of the family.

TOUGH TOPICS

Two topics that prove extremely sensitive between many couples are money and sex. Some men as well as some women simply cannot bring themselves to talk about their sex relationship to one another at all. If that is true, probably the best thing to do is simply to accept that circumstance and respect it rather than harangue the partner about it. Of course, it would be even better if a change could be accomplished, but it is really true that for some people such conversation is psychologically impossible.

The money topic is sensitive especially because it is easy for either husband or wife to feel that the other is at fault because there is not enough money. The discussion quickly becomes emotional, because in our society so much of life depends on money and also because guilt feelings are quickly roused since the use of money is a matter of judgment. But you need to discuss money. The many options of how money is to be handled, what bills to make or pay, what priorities of expenditure should be considered, and what avenues of income are open—all these questions you should discuss.

If you really want to communicate, you need trust in one another's good will, but you also need to understand one another's language and nonverbal signals. Otherwise your words will veer off into emotional display, or you will respond with the silent treatment or plunge into independent, and consequently inconsiderate, action. You can handle upsetting questions by discussion if you are confident that your partner is as concerned for the common good as you are.

COMMUNICATING ABOUT RELIGION

So far little has been said about one vital area of communication, namely, religion. In marriage you will do well to talk to one another about your understanding of God's message, your faith in Jesus Christ, and your application of religious values to your own relationship, to the daily decisions of life, and to your community responsibilities. When children come into your life, remember that it is in the home that the primary communication of religious values and practices takes place.

If there are religious books or pictures in the home, a cross on the wall, or mailings from the church, how these are treated, commented on, or explained can have influence on both adults and children. Even more important are the prayers at mealtime and bedtime, the reading of the Bible stories, and the response to one another's questions or comments on moral issues. Often the unguarded word or action says more than the formal presentation of a doctrine. The example of trust in God, of forgiveness and kindness, and of respect for biblical commands conveys to one another a deeper perception of spiritual reality than formal instruction. Usually it is necessary, though, to provide specific times and ways for religious communication and not trust entirely to casual situations even in the home. This is one of the reasons for home devotions.

PROBLEMS IN COMMUNICATION

When there is a barrier to communication between husband and wife, it should be recognized as serious. Just as it would be foolish to ignore an illness and hope that it will simply go away, so also with a barrier to communication. It is a serious problem that requires treatment. If your home remedies do not resolve the problem, professional help should be sought. Otherwise sulking, outbursts of temper, silent treatments, escape routines or even violence or infidelity become the alternative.

For good communication in marriage you must be able to assign proper weight and import to what is being said. In intimate conversation where all sorts of ideas are sent up as trial balloons, do not take everything with deadly seriousness. On the other hand, some seemingly offhand or light comments can be intended to reveal a distress or desire so deep the person dare not risk offering it as a serious comment. It takes considerable experience with one another and sensitivity to one another's needs for you to know just what is being communicated. But isn't it true, after all, that part of the essence of marriage is commitment to deep concern for what the other feels, needs, and wants?

If you have this concern, communication becomes easier and the intended meaning is understood from what may be awkwardly stated. The salt of good humor will help keep communication going. Add a little spice to your conversation by frequent touches of the kind of humor your spouse learns to expect. Like companionship, communication in marriage offers something precious that is an effective antidote to loneliness and alienation. Marriage is for two, and communication is one of the means for connecting them meaningfully.

THINGS TO CONSIDER

1. Why does communication stop between husbands and wives?
2. What kind of verbal assurances are commonly sought and needed by the wife? By the husband?
3. Is it important in marriage to give one another notice of tentative consideration of plans even before a final decision is needed? Why?
4. Is this true: "Husbands tend to become silently jealous when a wife's actions involve her with others"?
5. Are "put-down jokes" permissible between husband and wife in public or private?
6. What are some means of nonverbal communication?
7. When does banter become insult?
8. What is there to talk about between husband and wife?
9. Why is money such a sensitive topic in marriage?
10. What role should television play in the home?

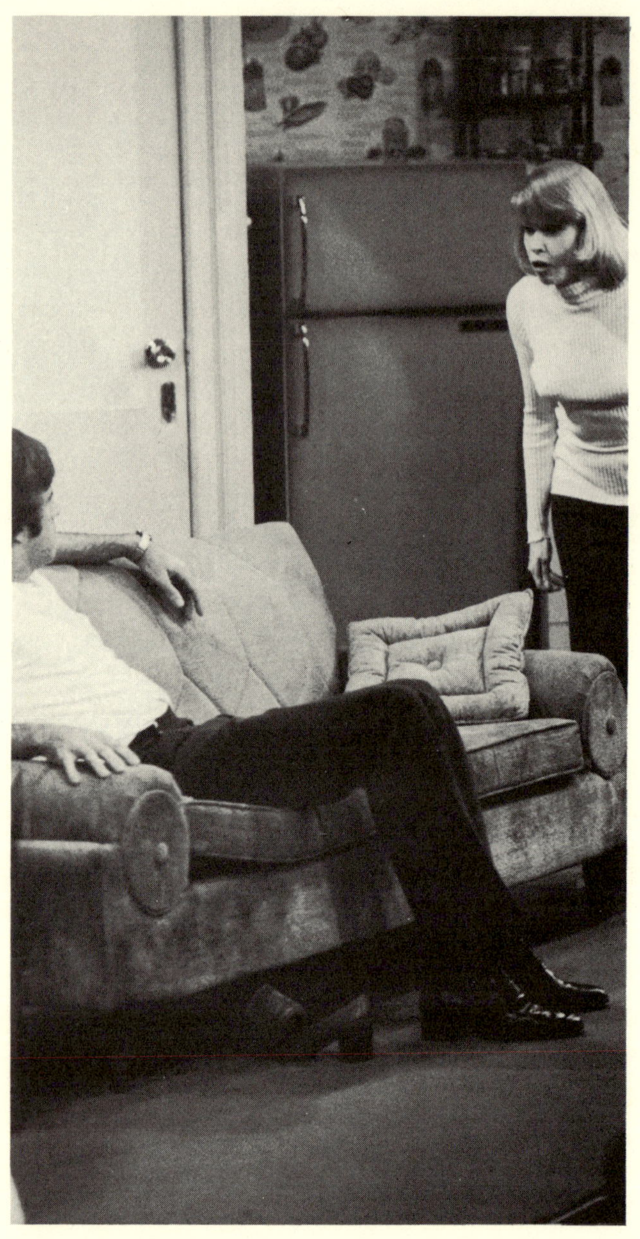

Five

Both Tension and Harmony Are Part of Marriage

Someone has said that to be free of tension a human being must be either dead or insane. Some tension is normal for human life at all ages. A marriage with no tension means a marriage with no contact or interaction. But tension is not a goal of marriage, harmony is.

Tensions between people who have tender feelings for one another usually come about through misunderstanding or misinterpretation. Of course, other tensions, mutually borne, will be thrust on you by circumstances.

The change from harmony to tension may come so suddenly in marriage that your tears may be inevitable. With effort, good listening, and evidence of mutual caring tensions can often be made productive.

Karen called her husband Ken at work one day because she was lonesome and because it had been a diffi-cult day for her with their two children. When Karen asked how things were going and started a leisurely, friendly chat, Ken asked, "Was there something you wanted, Karen? Why did you call?"

Karen was hurt. Just the night before everything seemed so good between them, and now her impulse to call Ken just to share a few minutes with him was met so abruptly. Tears came to her eyes, but she swallowed hard and said, "No, nothing special. I guess I was just lonesome for you."

"That's nice, Karen, but for crying out loud, I'm working," Ken replied. "I'll see you later when I get home. O.K.?"

Karen could hardly muster the good-bye, but somehow she managed, hung up the phone, and then sat in her kitchen and cried.

Such a juxtaposition of pleasant harmony and sudden tension is common in marriage. For the relationship between husband and wife includes so much—from romantic, intimate moments to routine household crises to major decisions about relatives, jobs, expenditures, and schedules. Both harmony and tension are frequent. It is important to accept tension as a normal part of human relationships but to consider how such tensions should be dealt with.

Both Karen's impulse to call Ken and his reaction are understandable to anyone who is married. In fact, the situation could just as easily have been reversed with Ken calling Karen and meeting a similar rebuff because her day was hectic and demanding. It isn't always the men who say the wrong thing in response to tenderness and reaching out.

If Ken took time to think later, he probably came home with flowers for Karen or at least with some kind words. If Karen had enough pleasant memories of other times with Ken, she may have been strong enough to welcome him tenderly when he came home and have a special dinner. Going the second mile to resolve tension brought about by misunderstanding can help you to make peace and reestablish harmony in a way that strengthens the relationship.

INSTANCES OF CARING

If you accept tension as something that will happen but need not destroy the security you feel in one another's love, tension can be productive. Otherwise, lacking security in one another's love, tension at home will seriously disturb your effectiveness at work or your freedom to pursue individual interests. Strive for enough trust between you so that you dare reach out to the other for emotional support. Recalling past instances of caring which the other has shown can enable you to turn away from the hurt caused by a thoughtless word or action.

For some, tensions may happen too frequently. One may be reaching out and the other turning away—out of disinterest, rejection, or other pressures. One spouse may also have a neurotic need for constant reassurance. It may also be that the episode reveals callousness, waning affection, or inability to sustain tender regard in your marriage relationship.

Some couples may need not only self-examination and mutual sharing of feelings but also professional, competent counseling. Many people simply do not understand the processes by which an intimate relationship can be established, nurtured, and controlled. If you need help in your relationship, seek it from your pastor or another competent marriage counselor. Through a series of consultations you may discover new options that fit your emotional patterns. New possibilities may require effort and guidance because they do not come easily or naturally to you. Ask the counselor not to take anything for granted because you are willing to hear even what may be obvious to him, since it may be a new alternative for you.

HARMONY IN MARRIAGE

Harmony in a marriage relationship depends largely on your commitment to one another. The expression of that commitment takes various forms. There must be commitment to companionship as your primary goal in your marital relationship so that both of you enjoy being together not only when you are doing something interesting but also when you are simply together in the ordinary routines of life. Sexual relationship, caring and sharing in a lifelong commitment, and ability to seek similar ideals and goals are also important for harmony in marriage.

When there is trust in one another's love and good will, whether life is rough or easy, harmony for you is only as far away as experience in living together. Harmony does not mean unbroken and unruffled quietude but sustained care and love, mutually expressed, in words and actions.

It needs to be said again that words of caring or affection without supporting action are a mockery of love and create tension. But caring actions without verbal expression are also insufficient for lasting harmony. God has given human beings the capacity to interpret themselves and their actions verbally, and they should do so. It is part of what it means to be human. It is also what

48

it takes to resolve tension and create harmony. Otherwise tensions are merely buried.

Misunderstanding is even more likely if words are not used. Occasionally someone will say, "Why do I have to keep saying I love you? Would I be here if I didn't? Don't my caring actions show I love you?"

There is a good point in this comment, of course, but words are important, too. Without words it is difficult to trust that love and good will prompted the actions.

Perfect harmony between a man and woman, however, is not possible even in marriage. It is foolish and artificial to pretend that no tensions or blocked feelings ever occur. It is not only inevitable but a sign of emotional health that feelings of anger, suspicion, resentment, hurt, and anxiety between husband and wife are acknowledged. Consequently, it is also important to discover how such tensions can constructively be resolved or utilized.

LOVE AND FORGIVENESS

The Christian assurance that God is merciful points the way. As through Jesus Christ we are assured of God's forgiveness, so husband and wife, having experienced God's mercy, can be ready to be forgiving to one another. This forgiveness does not mean the quick and easy "I'm sorry" and the equally glib "It doesn't matter. Forget it." Forgiveness involves the recognition that a real wrong was done but that nevertheless the injury will be accepted and absolved. It will no longer stand as a barrier. A reconciliation of love and forgiveness has taken place.

Tensions need more than forgiveness, though, to be used constructively. Tensions are also warning signals for areas of life that need attention. When these signals flash, try to understand one another's hopes or motives so that you can agree to alternative actions which satisfy both reasonably well. Almost always life offers alternatives.

A spirit of forgiveness between wife and husband enables them to deal with the many tensions of everyday life in the most wholesome way. Work to make that spirit mutual. Always try to determine the cause of the tension. The most obvious answers may be only superficial. If the tension threatens the marital relationship or if it is persistently recurring, both husband and wife should seek the help of a pastor or other counselor so that the rift may be healed through correct diagnosis and treatment.

OTHER TENSIONS

Other common tensions of varying seriousness are caused by young wives overly dependent on their mothers, by emotional claims of relatives that seem unreasonable to one spouse or the other, by sexual habits or desires, by shortage of income or excessive spending, by dissatisfaction with living arrangements, by disagreements over children, or by serious differences over what is important in life.

Tension is part of life. But it should not be left untended. Harmony should be dominant in married life. You will be able to stand a great deal of pressure, anxiety or pain in other areas of life if your life together as husband and wife is full of joy, caring, love, and meaning. If these elements are lacking in marriage, it is likely that you will also have considerable conflict, anxiety, or frustration in other areas of your life.

If husband and wife can take religion seriously, commit themselves to Jesus Christ as Savior and Lord, pray together at mealtime and bedtime, and give attention to Christian values and attitudes for themselves and for their children, then harmony between them is much more likely to be strong and lasting. These experiences together also provide a secure base for meeting tensions constructively so long as you are realistic enough to acknowledge tensions between yourselves and patient enough to search deeper than superficial causes and solutions for the tensions.

Harmony and tension are continuing experiences in a good marriage, and both need thoughtful attention to accomplish good in the lives of husband and wife. Few things in life are more beautiful or enrich life more than a harmonious marriage. The peace, security, and vitality such a relationship can give people supply abundant reason to thank God.

THINGS TO CONSIDER

1. Is tension normal?
2. What is the significance in marriage when one reaches out and the other turns away?
3. Can the need for reassurance become neurotic?
4. Define harmony.
5. What is the basic ingredient for harmony in a marriage?
6. Why are words so important to express caring when actions are positive?
7. Is it possible to have a marriage without any tensions?
8. What is the nature of forgiveness between husband and wife?
9. How does religion promote harmony in marriage?

Six

Relatives Are a Mixed Blessing

Family ties are created not only by blood relationship but also by sharing significant experiences. When you are married, make your life together an expression of the best in family ties. Mother shouldn't smother, but neither does putting your husband or wife first in human affection mean that you must no longer allow mother to influence your life. There is something wholesome about family ties that are close without being demanding or constrictive.

Often an unhappy pattern of the past threatens this bond or makes it unwelcome. Often a couple's first serious quarrel will have something to do with relatives.

It was Rick and Tracey's second Thanksgiving together. The first one had been just a little short of disaster.

Last year they had accepted the invitation from Rick's folks to have Thanksgiving dinner with them at noon. Then Rick decided to go pheasant hunting in the morning, and he and his partner traveled farther and hunted longer than they intended so that Rick didn't get home until almost 12:30.

By the time they got to his mother's dinner table, she was upset because everything was late and not perfect as she had planned. To top it off, Tracey's folks had called Thursday morning and said they knew that Tracey and Rick were having dinner at his folks but couldn't they stop over about 3:00 before Uncle John and Aunt Susie left to go back to Dayton? After all, Uncle John and Aunt Susie had been really good to them at the time of the wedding.

So Rick's folks were unhappy because Rick and Tracey rushed off, and Tracey's folks were a little tense because they didn't get there till 3:30 and Uncle John was one to leave on schedule.

That was last year. This year the young couple had turned down invitations from both sets of parents and decided to eat their own Thanksgiving turkey at home. To give themselves plenty of time in case Rick's hunting got late again, they decided to eat at midafternoon and ask some friends to drop in at early evening.

Everything worked out reasonably well until they were just finishing their meal when Tracey's folks "stopped by," as they said, but stayed on and on. At about 5:00 Rick's folks came, too. Then Tracey had to explain that they were expecting friends about 7:00, but the folks were welcome to stay. Of course, they didn't, but the mood under which they left showed they felt hurt and didn't understand.

Relationships with relatives could be clarified for Tracey and Rick if they would follow a few basic, but not easy, steps. First, there would have to be an understanding between Tracey and Rick themselves on how much involvement with family each desired. Next, they should clarify for each set of parents that though their loyalty and love to them would be secure, they also needed friends and activities apart from either family. Finally, Tracey and Rick should be sure to cultivate friends who are not relatives.

GOOD INTENTIONS

Many a bride has lifted her eyes with a shy mixture of surprise and hope when she heard in premarriage counseling that relatives are often a problem. The surprise comes apparently because someone dares to voice a feeling she has had: that those who are so dear to her and toward whom she has strong feelings of loyalty should also be a source of tension.

Why do relatives prove a threat to the even flow of wedding preparation by bride and groom or later to their marriage relationship? It is not, as stated, because tension is what relatives intend. Nearly all parents intend only good for the happy couple. If bride and groom remember that parents and other relatives want to help them, they will find their suggestions much easier to deal with.

Most important of all, in this respect, is for bride and groom to share privately with one another what they themselves want. If you can agree as bride and groom on a certain idea for the wedding, parents may say, "These kids nowadays; one never knows what they will come up with," but they will probably go along with it. But if you two indicate that you cannot agree or have not made up your mind, then the pressure will mount, and all sorts of forceful suggestions will be made.

Even something as simple as drawing up a list of guests to the wedding can create tensions. Parents often want to include persons the couple doesn't even know. Likewise tensions with relatives easily arise over what is to be worn at the wedding and where the reception is to be held. After marriage parental counsel, especially if it borders on control, is not always well received. That does not mean counsel should not be given. Rather it means that all involved, the couple, the parents, and other well-meaning relatives, must recognize that part of marriage for the newlyweds is the right to make their own decisions—and bear the consequences. You will have to learn how to let parents know tastefully and lovingly that personal decisions are your own.

Parents might take the caution, however, not to be easily offended when their advice is not taken, and newlyweds might take courage from having to differ with them in the thought that this tension is normal. So long as love and loyalty prevail the transition to thoughtful independence can be accomplished.

Of course, a bride and groom (or young wife and husband) who are sensible and loving will want to give serious consideration to advice from parents and other older adults. Experience and thought should have given older adults a perspective which may benefit the young. But the two of you should always discuss the question and make your decision in such a way that the bond of privacy between you is not broken, and that the decision freely becomes your own.

NEW PRIORITIES

Marriage creates a revised structure of priorities in relationship. Therefore you need to give careful thought to the fact that after marriage the first human claim on each will always spring from the spouse. In the chain of human priorities the husband now comes first in the wife's thought, ahead of parents and, later, even of children. And for the husband his wife now takes precedence over parents, boss, friends, and anyone else.

The bond between you is not chiefly one of law but of love. And where love is the bond, its claim sometimes yields priority willingly to the claims of someone else who is also dear. But such yielding should be recognized as an exception to the proper order, an exception of necessity or by loving consent, but still an exception.

Many practical implications for the way marriage is lived flow out of the recognition of the changed priorities. The importance and practicality of Jesus' words: "Therefore shall a man leave father and mother and cleave unto his wife" become clearly evident. If her husband is offered a job in another place apart from her parents, the wife who remembers that her first loyalty now stands with her husband will find it easier to move with peace and anticipation.

In fact, it is usually an advantage if a newly-married couple does not live too near either parental home. Almost any sacrifice of convenience is worthwhile to enable newly-married persons to live elsewhere than with one of the parental families. Another rule of thumb is that you should not commit yourselves to patterns of visiting parents or grandparents which are so frequent or so inflexible that you will come to resent them. It may be pleasant for a while to have your weekends in parental homes and to enjoy the security, comfort, and cuisine they have achieved. But when such constant visiting patterns become firm and expected, they will in time become not only burdensome but also inhibiting for all concerned.

COMMITMENTS

The same holds true for holiday celebrations. It is great to have Christmas, Thanksgiving, or other festival times with relatives. But if you are not careful, you will soon establish inflexible commitments to have Christmas at one house or the other. That may suit some people, but for others it will prove to be more of a chore than a pleasure.

The other side of the coin for newlyweds is that newlyweds should not cut themselves off from relatives. Sometimes family life at home has been so filled with bitterness or conflict that the young person getting married desires nothing more than simply to be free of relatives. Such a course is fraught with emotional dynamite. The ties of blood are very strong, and you cannot deliberately sever them without severe emotional damage to your personality. At least the courtesies of an occasional note, a birthday or Christmas card, or an inquiry about parental well-being should be maintained even when relationships are strained or disruptive.

Furthermore, for most families, relatives can be a real blessing. Being with people whose habits and outlook are similar to your own and who have known each other through years of personality development can give you a feeling of comfortableness and ease. Such security is not easily achieved with more recent acquaintances. Also the sense of your own identity is strengthened by having relatives who link life to its origins and give a generational perspective on both past and future. In times of prolonged problems it is family and relatives who are most likely to supply support, emotional and financial. Friends usually help first, but relatives often help the longest.

As in many situations between husband and wife, relationships with relatives should be something you consider, experiment with, and on which you reach a compromise. To put it another way, as husband and wife, you should share your feelings and thoughts, trust one another's good will and that of your parents, appeal to God in prayer for patience and understanding, and then together, make decisions and live with them bravely and hopefully.

THINGS TO CONSIDER

1. Why and how do relatives create tension between a bride and groom (or husband and wife)?
2. Discuss: "After marriage the first human claim on each will always spring from the spouse."
3. Why is it important to realize that the bond between husband and wife is both one of law and one of love?
4. Should a wife always move willingly to where a husband's work takes him?
5. How can holidays with relatives be kept a choice rather than a duty?
6. Why is cutting oneself off from close relatives "emotional dynamite"?

Seven

Use Money Wisely

The wealthiest people in the world are not necessarily the happiest. Few really poor people are happy either. Small wonder that Solomon prayed to have what was appropriate for him rather than to have either poverty or riches.

Money is a tool. Its value lies in what it can buy. For some people storing away money becomes a goal; for others money should be converted to goods or services as speedily as possible. In the previous chapter we looked at what can constructively be done with families and relatives; in this chapter we look at finances.

Karen had problems with money. Somehow it seemed that attractive goods always cost more than she could afford to pay. So she used credit and charge cards.

It wasn't long before Kenny, her husband, couldn't meet the monthly bills. He was very much in love with

Karen and thought her extravagance was just a mistake. Perhaps she didn't realize how much she was spending. He told her, almost jokingly, that if she kept this up they would be bankrupt before they were married a year.

Karen's buying was compulsive, however, and though she held herself back for a few months, she couldn't resist the impulse any longer. Once again the credit account soared. This time she took the bills when they came in the mail and hid them. Somehow she thought a way would open up so the bills could be paid.

The next month the bills came again with a stern warning about what would happen if at least the minimum installment were not paid. Karen was frightened but resourceful—though a little foolish. She asked her father for enough money to pay something on all bills by telling him that they were short and she didn't want to tell Ken he wasn't bringing home enough.

Eventually, of course, Karen and Kenny had a rough time facing what was happening. They dealt with it by getting rid of their credit cards except one, which Ken carried, for gasoline for the car. A counselor also helped them set up a budget which covered their regular expenses and gave Karen a limited amount each month to spend as she chose. Fortunately Karen recognized her need for help, and she and Ken tried to be open and loving toward one another.

EXERCISING CHOICE

Tensions are part of human life from birth to the grave. Only the dead, the utterly foolish, and those who have sought release from tension in emotional illness, alcohol, or drugs, can be unaware of tension. It is not the tension itself that is bad, unless it reaches inordinate proportions, or if we deal with it in unwholesome ways.

Ordinarily, when people feel the tension of hunger, they should eat. When they are tired, they should sleep. When tensions of fear, anger, laughter, restlessness, or any others come to people, the first thing to realize is that there are various ways to relieve the tension. Human beings exercise choice.

When angry feelings mount, it is not necessary to shout, to strike out, or to use profanity. There are other choices. Kenny had to make choices when he faced Karen's credit charges. He made sane and loving choices rather than impulsively yielding only to feeling. Different situations in life and different goals, like different temperaments and different training, will encourage varying choices. Remember that you have a choice.

We should not forget that we are human. Though this means on the one hand that you are prone to morally weak and reprehensible choices, it also means on the other hand that you are capable of noble and unselfish choices. Christians testify to the need for the grace of God. Human beings have—and should have—a sense of guilt, but the sense of guilt can be relieved and removed by the confidence that God is merciful. We know that he is merciful because his Son, Jesus Christ, has atoned for our sin and guilt and cleansed us of our sin before God. That trust in a merciful God can not only free us from guilt, but it can also make our thoughts, words, and actions good in intention as well as in effect.

What does any of this have to do with the tension of finances? In our use of money we recognize most easily our innate selfishness and also our capacity to do good. The exercise of that capacity is a reason for praising the power of God who changes us. In the use of money, as in life generally, your priorities are important. That is part of the tension between husband and wife over finances: people have different priorities.

Even falling in love, even pledging lifelong loyalty to one another in marriage, does not by itself change your priorities in the use of money. Accepting this tension at the outset can help you learn patience and practice conversation about the use of money.

PARENTAL PRIORITIES

Finances are one area of life where parents and other older adults can help young people least by their counsel. That does not mean that parental priorities are wrong for themselves. What they want out of life in terms of financial security, income, pleasure that money can buy, and comforts may be quite suitable for them. How they use their money to honor God, help people, or achieve worthwhile goals should be decisively established at their age. But how parents see the conserving and use of finances may differ radically from the priorities by which their children live.

Many older adults established their patterns of financial management at a time much different from now. An economy of scarcity rather than abundance, a time of war rather than days of peace, being thrown on one's own early in life rather than being subsidized or supported through college—all these affect one's financial bias. If you will listen to your parent's words, but not take them as either ridiculous or decisive, you may find parental counsel useful. But it would be a mistake for newlyweds either to seek to compete financially with the way their parents live or to imitate the parental pattern simply because of parental financial success.

For most people finances continue to be a problem throughout life. It is important to recognize this so that expectations for reaching easy street do not become the root for dissatisfaction. Many people are short of money all the time so that an unexpected expense, as trivial as a pair of shoes or as major as extensive car repairs can be a catastrophe. If you learn to accept this problem as a fact of ordinary existence, it may save you from undue panic or impulsive borrowing.

Probably one of the most important and most useful ideas to accept in handling family finances is that there is no one best or sure way to success. There are many different good—and bad—ways to handle money in the home. It will be helpful if you do not set an inflexible pattern too early. A husband who declares the day after the wedding, "As long as we're married, I'll make the financial decisions and handle the money in this family," is not only presumptuous but also foolish. The bride who accepts such a pronouncement meekly is just as foolish.

FLEXIBILITY

In handling finances early in marriage it is best to keep some flexibility. The husband may start by writing all the checks and keeping the financial records, but he may discover that his wife has a better head for it and is more faithful in little things. It may be a relief—and an act of wisdom—for him to be able to turn these matters over to his wife without losing face.

Perhaps nothing shows the constant flux in economic thinking and patterns more than the choice to use cash or credit. We have moved largely from a cash to a credit society. Sometimes this shift is noticeable in a pronounced way between generations of the same family—probably because emotional patterns relating to money were conditioned differently by culture or environment. Sometimes, too, attitudes toward spending and saving, investments and ownership, change rapidly so that people not separated greatly by age still show wide variance in economic patterns. How patterns change within the same vocational category can be seen plainly among farmers. Once farmers were great cash or short-term credit buyers, but the necessity for huge investments in machinery, fertilizers, and land purchases has involved almost all of them in an unending dependence on credit and borrowing.

No one pattern of financial management is best for everyone. Some still live, either by necessity or choice, largely on a cash basis. They do not buy (except perhaps a home or a car) unless they can pay cash. If you go largely on a cash basis, you will start out with used furniture, a rented apartment, and an older car. Such an approach may be very wise.

RISK APPROACH

But if as newlyweds you decide to buy a new home, fill it with new furniture, and drive a late model car, all largely on credit, that is not to say you are being foolish—if you realize what you are doing. You have then taken a different risk approach to life and obligated yourselves to use almost all of your paychecks for time payments. It will probably also mean that the new wife will have to hold a job outside the home for some years.

The way to stretch one's income the farthest and to feel most satisfied with how money is spent is to set up a comprehensive budgeting system and follow it with careful accounting of every dollar of income and expenditure. Unfortunately, few people are able to set up and maintain such a system over a period of years. Therefore most people settle for a modification of this plan. They realize that it is immediate disaster to spend money needed for housing, food, utilities, and insurance on having fun. Anyone who flaunts this rule of thumb in financial management by spending for fun or a fling money needed for basics is on the way to serious financial trouble.

Whatever pattern of finances you follow, you should remember to establish priorities. Using money for church or charitable causes should not wait until you have more income than you need. You may very well never see such a time. Setting aside a specific percentage of your income to give to church and charity, out of love to God and people, will add satisfaction and meaning to life. But, above all, it should be done because God wills it and accepts such actions as reverent worship.

Never should the mere accumulation of money or property, either for security or for comfort or display, become the main goal of life. That way lies disaster. When people are too hungry for money or for what it will buy, the love of money becomes the root of all kinds of evil. Those who have eyes to see will observe this result all around them in the lives of people they know.

Money itself is only a tool, of itself neither good nor bad. If you will exercise some prudence, learn from your financial mistakes, and be content with what you can reasonably hope for, financial concerns will not easily become a major problem in your marriage. If other people can make it, you can probably do just as well.

A combination of faith in God and personal attention to prudence and duty can help you use money wisely.

THINGS TO CONSIDER

1. Are credit cards a blessing or a curse?
2. Discuss some of the choices we have to relieve tension when angry.
3. What are the two directions human beings can take in making choices about how to deal with tensions?
4. Is there generally a difference in how parents think money should be used and conserved and how the next generation views the same questions?
5. Should the husband handle all the finances?
6. What is household budgeting? Is it useful?
7. Where do church contributions fit in?
8. When does money become the root of all evils?

Eight

Check Number One Priorities

In the previous chapter on finances, reference was made to the importance of priorities in the use of money. When we now speak of values, we deal with priorities in an even more extended and important way.

Kris and Scott seemed to be getting farther and farther apart in their marriage. Sometimes it seemed that all that held them together was the convenience of being married for bills, meals, and social participation and with the fact that the physical part of their sex relationship was good. But they bickered a lot, spent much time in separate activities, and agreed on fewer and fewer plans and hopes.

One day Kris said bluntly, "Why are we staying together, Scott? We don't really like each other anymore, and it's a long time since I could honestly say to you, 'I love you.'"

Scott had to agree that the question was in order, though he felt no need to end the marriage. Long ago he had found his friendships and his social and cultural stimulation elsewhere. The best he could reply was, "But what about our two children?"

Scott and Kris had waited too long before trying to do something about their relationship. They no longer trusted one another's real concern or interest in the other. Even actions that came from thoughtfulness or attempt at change were misinterpreted as evidence of manipulation or outward show. Their marriage ended in divorce which bore a facade of friendliness but hid deep disillusionment and frustration.

Of all the ordinary and predictable tensions in a marriage, the most serious and potentially the most dangerous is over values. Values are what is important to a person as a goal, attitude, or idea. The greatest red flag in a marriage relationship is waving wildly when one or both of the partners in marriage consistently feel that the other no longer cares what the partner wants. When it seems that the partners think only selfishly and self-centeredly with little regard for the spouse's feelings, hopes, or needs, the couple should seek professional counseling. It is unlikely that they will resolve their differences unaided.

CHOOSING NUMBER ONE

Values are, in fact, the moral and spiritual structure of priorities by which we build our lives. When we use the term values, we mean something more than good sense. Good sense is important too, and it is needed to make wise choices, financial and otherwise. Good sense means the ability to judge the relative worth and importance of what is under consideration in terms of personal benefit and general welfare. It involves practical judgment, like whether a specific car is a better buy than another, whether today is the day to quit one's job, and whether more is gained by eating at home or eating out.

Ordinarily, such choices do not involve moral or spiritual factors, but deal with what is wise rather than with what is good. You will, however, face other choices which are primarily moral or spiritual in meaning and impact. They include what is called religion and, therefore, also involve the Christian faith and its various church branches. Part of what we think about under values is church affiliation: is it important and how does it affect your view of marriage and the integrity of your lives?

Values are broader in scope, however, than church attendance or deciding which of two denominations you should choose. Such matters are important and should be discussed and decided before marriage, but they are by no means the whole story. Couples who belong to the same denomination may still have considerable difference in value structure and therefore considerable tension in this area of life.

Some newlyweds are taken by surprise when such differences in value surface even though they have similar cultural and religious backgrounds. When there is similarity in background, the conflict is not usually head-on; for example, one does not say, God is all-important, and the other, God does not matter. The conflict tends rather to be one of difference in a scale of value. For instance, the young wife may say, "But you weren't completely honest with me about why you didn't come home just when you said you would." To which the husband, who gives complete honesty a different rank in the scale of values, may reply, "The reason I didn't tell you everything is you would have gotten upset if I had told you this fellow at work wanted me to stop by and see his new boat after work. So I just said something came up at work. What's the big deal?"

It isn't necessarily that the husband thinks it is all right to be dishonest, to lie or cheat, it is just that honesty in the sense his wife conceives it does not rank number one in his scale in such a situation. It is more important, as he sees it, to spare his wife unnecessary distress or hurt feelings, so long as no one is deliberately harmed by it.

VALUE-TENSIONS OCCUR

If tensions about values occur even when people have more or less the same religious undergirding, surely a consideration of values, what is ultimately important to each, should be part of serious courtship. Tensions occur when one partner discovers that some value held dear is scoffed at by the other. Especially is this signal a warning for you when it involves values like reverence, thrift, obedience to law, respect for parents, self-control, fidelity, industriousness, truth, honesty, or compassion.

This matter of values often is the issue that ends a marriage. When finally one or the other in a marriage comes to the conclusion, "We have nothing in common. I can't respect the other. I can't stand any more ridicule or irresponsibility," saving such a marriage will be extremely difficult. In a traditional marriage ritual there are many commitments that have to do with values as well as to the permanence of the marriage vow. Unfortunately these values are not always heard with utmost seriousness; or perhaps the hope rules, because of romantic love, that the other will change so that uniformity of values will happen automatically. No confidence more often turns out to be an illusion than this hope.

PRIORITIES CAN BE MODIFIED

Human beings do change. One of the basic tenets of Christianity is that every human being can and must change radically. But unfortunately, when it comes to values, the emotional pattern of response is set deeply so early in life that major changes are difficult. The implications of these patterns in your life must be reckoned with, even though the Christian beliefs about conversion, sanctification, and Christian growth remain valid.

In this area of life which is so essential, sharing in marriage is necessary. If a couple never talks about God, about what counts most in life, or about why this action or attitude is right or wrong, trouble lies ahead.

In values, as in so much of life, it is important to share with other human beings, to listen to the expressions which the community gives of its standards, and, above all, to depend on God's Word and sacraments for direct help. Marriage gives a unique opportunity of trust and love to open oneself to another human being for growth and change even in such a deep-seated area as values.

Differences in values may be in relatively trivial areas of life or in the most basic. Even minor habits, like whether the toothpaste tube is squeezed from the end or the middle or whether the cap is always replaced or left off, can be disconcerting. In more important matters the tension mounts. For instance, a common difference in values between partners in marriage has to do with time—when to arise in the morning, when to retire, how punctually to eat meals, and whether being on time is important.

How shall value differences be reconciled? The first attempt is usually persuasion: one tries to convince the other that a given view is really better or more important than another. This approach is often not successful. Another way of getting at the difference is either by bargaining or compromise. One may say, "I'll give in on this matter if you will change in another." Or one may offer compromise by saying, "I'll relent a little in one direction if you relent a little from the other, so that we meet in the middle ground." But there are issues too important for bargaining or compromise. For these it is necessary to realize that you cannot have very many important value differences that are irreconcilable and expect to have a happy marriage. They should be examined before you enter upon marriage.

REENFORCING VALUES

In the marriage ritual praying for and with one another and being aware always of the eternal implications of life are emphasized. A newly-married couple should identify with a Christian congregation, and being faithful in responsibility for the work of the parish adds to the strength of the relationship. In fact, there are three points in life when adults are likely to make a fresh start in church relationship: one is when they marry, another is when their first child enters Sunday school, and the third is when they move to a new community. If you do not make a fresh start at these times, you may never do it.

In the home, too, prayers together at mealtime and other sharing of religious life should be started at once. It is not wise or good for you to hold off religious participation in a church until children come nor should religious participation be built only on the needs of children when they do come.

Life in marriage without awareness of the power and love of God lacks true perspective. The input into a marriage which comes from regular attendance at church worship services and Bible classes is invaluable. By being there together both partners have a common reference point for discussing and deciding what values are determined by the message God gives us in the Bible.

THINGS TO CONSIDER

1. What is meant by "priorities"?
2. Why is it dangerous in a troubled marriage to wait too long before seeking counseling?
3. Which is the most serious tension in marriage? Why?
4. What is the difference between judgments made according to "values" and judgments made through "good sense"?
5. How important are the following to each of you: being on time, getting up early, saying prayers together, being open with each other?
6. Why is it the question of values that so often brings a marriage to its breaking point?
7. Should husband and wife discuss the reasons for their personal value-structure?
8. How shall value differences be reconciled?
9. How does church membership affect one's value structure?

Nine

Sexual Relationship Strengthens Unity

Couples come in all sorts of shapes, sizes, and appearances. There is no accounting for combinations in marriage on the basis of physical characteristics alone. The sexual attraction of a man and woman for each other, for all the changing styles and moods of sex appeal, depends on much more than physical measurements.

A man and woman are often drawn to one another in what is called romantic love in a way that conflicts with good judgment. Small wonder that the biblical author of Proverbs lists as one of the four things "too mysterious for me to understand" the phenomenon of a man and a woman falling in love.

It is important to realize that one can fall in love rather easily, especially, but not only, in youth. Most people have been "in love" with various people before they choose one as their husband or wife. Also after marriage it may come as a shock to you to find yourself strangely attracted to someone other than your mate. Such feelings must be dealt with. One of the chief things to keep in mind is to avoid dalliance, flirting with the danger by allowing affection to grow through repeated association and expressions of tenderness. It is also important to remember that marriage is a choice.

Human beings are monogamous not by nature or instinct but by reasoned choice and moral commitment. By getting married each consents to a lifelong bond in which love, caring, sharing, faithfulness, and sexual attention is sought and given. Furthermore, these are promised exclusively to one another in marriage. Husband and wife promise to treat one another and to care for one another as they do no one else.

THE TEST OF RELATIONSHIP

In the most specific sense this applies to the sexual relationship. Perhaps that is why matters related to sex become the most common test and tribute of a marriage relationship.

Chuck and Tammie had needed marriage counseling for a long time. Their religious conviction made them fear divorce and their two young children also held them back. Otherwise they were ready to give up on their marriage.

Their problems were many, but their sexual relationship and their differences over money became the chief points at issue. Finally, in desperation they went to see the pastor. What could be done? Wasn't it really better for everyone if the marriage were dissolved?

They talked of many things, some that happened years ago. The pastor guided them with questions so that the tension between them didn't make them simply say, "We don't love each other anymore." The pastor tried to help them see what had originally drawn them to each other, what their hopes had been, and where the root of their differences lay.

One strong area of conflict which they themselves recognized was sex. Chuck had withdrawn from sexual relationship with his wife completely for the last six months, and before that sexual intimacy was rare for at least another year. Tammie felt bitter, frustrated, and hurt over this circumstance. She couldn't understand it, and she felt cheated. Also lately she wondered whether Chuck had another woman.

By careful exploration of their basic feelings about marriage and about each other under the pastor's patient probing, Tammie and Chuck came to renewed determination to try to make their marriage work. A series of sessions with the pastor helped them realize there was much that could be done to change the pattern of alienation that had developed between them. They had been too intent on independently doing whatever they felt like.

COMMON TENSIONS

Such sexual tensions have become relatively common in recent years. The roots are varied, but one of the factors is the changed sexual self-understanding of women and the threatening effect this has had on the male. Some thought should be given to the new equality between men and women when sexual roles are considered.

In spite of all the emphasis on verbal sharing in our society and all the sex education in our schools, many people still do not realize the full import of the word *relationship*. Human beings require communication for any strong and meaningful relationship. Furthermore, the sexual act in marriage has both a strong emotional and also an important social significance.

Those who marry need to remember that their sexual natures and their sexual acts contribute to, express, or detract from their relationship to one another. Such realization makes it easier, too, to see why adultery and promiscuity are so destructive and dangerous to the human character as well as to the marriage bond.

Occasionally both men and women who are married, but more frequently women, do not reckon with the necessity of the sexual relationship in marriage. This does not mean that never could a marriage continue without the sexual act, for it does. But deprivation is dangerous and unnatural unless it be when desire and capability wanes in old age. The Apostle Paul indicates this danger in 1 Corinthians 7:5 stating, "Do not deny yourselves to each other, unless you first agree to do so for a while in order to spend your time in prayer; but then resume normal marital relations."

There is not only romantic desire, physical benefit, and emotional communication involved in the sexual act in marriage, there is also the recognition of routine and wholesome obligation to one another. It presents another instance of thinking of the partner's need and desire ahead of one's own. Some Christians do not seem to be aware of the counsel Paul gives. Even more surprising is the discovery that some husbands and wives do not know that they cannot legally deny one another the sexual act for any length of time without evident physical or other compelling reasons.

All of us should remember, however, that the sexual

relationship in marriage ought to be more than the fulfillment of an obligation or the claiming of a right. It
should be far more spontaneous, expressing love, intimacy, and generous concern for the other as well as
satisfying one's own desire and pleasure. Perhaps in
this most intimate, enjoyable, and repeated action the
accomplishing of the biblical reality that the two shall
be one flesh is most clearly evident.

MUTUALITY IN SEX

When the sex organ of the male penetrates that of the
female in a prolonged, loving marital relationship, the
resulting ecstasy, physical as it is, becomes also deeply
emotional. Because of this mutuality of effort and response, the sexual act can serve to anchor affection in an
event of self-surrender by each. Both husband and wife
become vulnerable emotionally in the sexual act. This
vulnerability is one reason why the sexual act so easily
becomes the most clearly identified battleground in
marital strife.

This is why the Scripture warns that a man who has
sexual relations with a prostitute makes himself one
with her. The emotional exploitation of prostitution or,
for that matter, all illicit sex results in callousness, conflict of loyalty, or disturbing guilt. Sex outside of marriage creates a world of illusion in contrast to the
wholesome reality of the marriage commitment.

The forgiveness gained for us by Jesus Christ applies
just as clearly and fully to adultery or fornication, when
repented of, as to any other sin. But the emotional
feeling of being forgiven for these transgressions does
not come easily. The stain and strain of sexual unfaith-
fulness or perversion is deep and strong. Often later

sexual relationships in marriage are colored by remembrance of past guilty experiences. In this matter too, husband and wife can help one another by patience, care, and love.

TENDERNESS COUNTS

Tenderness and true regard for the other person should be sought and cherished in the sexual act in marriage. The biological and emotional urge and desire for a sexual relationship are obviously good and useful, and we should never draw the conclusion that all sexual excitement, arousal, or stimulation are sinful. They become detrimental only according to misuse or when sexual arousal focuses the mind on forbidden ground.

Since the first advantage of marriage is trusting companionship and mutual help, the sexual relationship and act should be seen too in that light. Sex is not something to be joked about, nor is it something grim. It is a God-given inclination and ability which he has endowed with great pleasure and sense of well-being in its practice between husband and wife. Furthermore God has chosen the sexual act as the means he uses for the procreation of children and the extension of the human race.

Although I do not subscribe to the idea that only the desire to have children validates the sexual act, I also would not want marriage partners to lose sight of this high and holy sharing with God in his creation. For this reason married people should examine their motives carefully and be cautious before they reject entirely the possibility of having children. (The preceding sentence is not to be read as a stricture against birth control or family planning itself. That is quite another question.)

Our time has set before married couples quite a different circumstance than that which faced generations long ago. We are in serious danger of world overpopulation. In previous ages there was obviously room for many more people, and it had to be assumed that many children born would never reach adulthood and that most adults would never reach what we consider to be old age. That does alter considerably the duty to have children in order to "be fruitful and multiply and replenish the earth."

One point that needs to be made briefly is that marriage does not by any means solve or resolve all sexual tension. A young man or woman who believes that after marriage he or she will no longer be tempted by unwholesome sexual fantasies is mistaken. Attractions of a surprisingly physical and sexual nature for persons other than husband or wife will occur, more frequently for some than others. Even a desperate frustration at not always being physically or emotionally satisfied sexually is possible. The essence of what it means to be human, to seek the will of God and cause good to prevail over evil by deliberate choice, continues to be essential also where sex is concerned in marriage.

WISE SEX

In general, so long as both married partners are at ease with it and nothing is forced on the other, almost any means of expressing their sexual relationship is not sinful within marriage. But not everything may be wise. Likewise some actions which may be useful, wholesome, and good if they occur occasionally can become disastrous or repulsive if they get to be the common means of fulfilling sexual acts.

Ordinarily not nearly so much depends on variety or refinement of technique in sexual encounter as depends on tenderness and genuine evidence of concern for the other. It is extremely useful also if you can communicate in words your sexual feelings, desires, and fears. When this is not possible emotionally that should also be incorporated into the tenderness and concern for one another and accepted.

It will be good for husband and wife never to taunt one another about sex or to criticize or joke about one another before others about their sexual relationship. You have been made one, and just as a wholesome individual does not humiliate himself before others, so husband and wife should refrain from words or actions which indicate ridicule or contempt.

The privacy of the relationship between husband and wife is to be cherished, not only in the area of sex but also in other intimate and revealing matters between them. For this reason and for others, people who are newly married should live apart from others, alone as a couple. When that is simply impossible, they should nevertheless establish and guard zealously places and times of complete privacy.

Finally, there is a simple principle which serves well as a guide to the sexual act in marriage. It may not always be possible and could certainly be misused as a rule, but it seems to have value as a principle: young couples in good health should relate in the sexual act as often as either one desires it. Circumstances may lay all sorts of strictures on this principle, but it is nonetheless a useful guide for the attitude of both husband and wife.

THINGS TO CONSIDER

1. Is it easy to "fall in love"?
2. What is meant by the statement: "Marriage is a choice"?
3. Is it true that "human beings are not monogamous by nature"?
4. What are some reasons why husband and wife withdraw from sex with one another?
5. Is the sexual relationship ever optional in marriage?
6. Why are both husband and wife emotionally "vulnerable" through the sexual act?
7. Discuss: "Sex outside of marriage creates a world of illusion in contrast to the wholesome reality of the marriage commitment."
8. Is it correct to say that only the desire to have children validates the sexual act?
9. Is it desirable for husband and wife to talk with one another about their sexual feelings or desires?
10. Discuss: "Young couples in good health should relate in the sexual act as often as either one desires it."

Ten

Be Good to One Another

Married life can be fun. If you will take time to watch what cheers your spouse or what brings a chuckle or a laugh, you can lighten many days with a little humor. Such exchange adds a lot to the daily pleasure of living together.

You will find, too, that little acts of thoughtfulness will be noticed and appreciated—and sometimes bring a word of thanks. Even little courtesies or an unexpected hug or a good cup of coffee offered at the appropriate moment add much to the bliss of married life.

Too many marriages are either grim or lifeless. Add a little sparkle to your relationship in a way that suits your personality. Sometimes the attempt will misfire and may even be misunderstood, but often it will draw you closer in a cheerful, delightful way.

The danger of taking one another for granted is

real in marriage, and effort must be made to avoid malaise. In marriage feelings are often an accumulation of little things, small slights or frequent courtesies, and the understanding or misunderstanding that grows often depends on incidents that are trivial by themselves.

Sandi was puzzled, hurt, and troubled. She had always tried to be a good wife. Bill's meals were seldom late. The children were always being looked after so they wouldn't "bother" him. The house was clean and comfortable, and she was rarely absent when he came home.

All this Bill expected of her, and she had always complied, finding her pleasure in life in being competent and in her children and church. She didn't have it easy, but Bill often reminded her that he worked hard, too, and that she was a lot better off than before she got married.

Now, however, Bill wasn't talking to her anymore, and he was irritable. Last night he left the house after dinner and didn't come back till after she had finally fallen asleep at 1:00. Not only that; the other day when one of the children had said how nice she looked in a new outfit she had made, Bill had laughed.

No wonder Sandi finally sought counsel. The ways and means to correct what had been wrong through 17 years of marriage would not be easy, and the present crisis in Bill's changed attitude would not make him easily receptive. For though he had always been difficult to live with and often inconsiderate of Sandi, in the past he had not been deliberately cruel.

A BASIC EXPRESSION

Sandi's case illustrates that in the marriage relationship longsuffering martyrs, even willing martyrs, are seldom appreciated by their spouses. Often they are even cheated on or deserted for more exciting company. Being good to one another is a basic expression of the commitment of marriage, but to make a happy marriage the attitude and action must be mutual. Marriage is for two.

Bill's action and attitude stemmed from an idea about marriage he had gained in childhood. His parents seldom spoke tenderly to one another, and his father had always come and gone as he pleased with little consideration for the plans of his wife or children.

The counselor found it necessary to meet with Bill separately for numerous sessions to which Bill consented only because he liked the counselor. Eventually he recognized that what he thought was the way every husband behaved did not work well in marriage today. Since he really loved Sandi but lacked skill in relating tenderly, some progress began to show when he made attempts to change. Sandi came to new security which made her more attractive to Bill than before.

In Ephesians 5:21 the Apostle Paul states a principle of tremendous importance for human relationships in marriage. In fact, his enunciation of the principle immediately precedes specific instructions to husbands and wives. He says, "Submit yourselves to one another because of your reverence for Christ." What is sought here is a subordination of self-interest out of concern for the spouse. As the wife is to ask what her husband wants, so the husband is to sacrifice himself in love for his wife. It is a mutual commitment.

Husband and wife are to seek an equality of personhood with respect for one another's dignity, conscience, and choice. It is an equality of love, wherein each thinks first of the other, not in a patronizing way, but recognizing intellect, will, and emotion. Before God maleness or femaleness is not of first importance, but awareness of relationship to God himself and to other people according to the circumstances and commitments of one's life.

Though marriage is not simply a contract between two persons who feel a need, a desire, and a hope in relation to one another, it is at least a contract. The marriage ritual traditionally speaks of "the serious responsibilities you are about to assume" in a way that sounds much like a contract. The two persons in the marriage covenant do agree, of their own will and consent, to specific attitudes and actions toward one another.

What marriage means is, of course, more than contractual. Love which cannot really be analyzed, which often defies logic, usually exists between a man and a woman when marriage is begun. In addition to similar interests and habits and dissimilar characteristics that attract, there is an indefinable bond between them that somehow makes their futures seem inescapably and happily intertwined. The love that leads to marriage is romantic, a little foolish, and most promising. But marriage is not only a matter of the heart but also of the head; love and good sense should agree on the choice of a marriage partner.

The choice made is of vital importance. One might say that of all the people one has loved, might love, or will in the future love, only one should be chosen as spouse. Your choice should be permanent, binding, and fruitful. It is a choice through which God joins the couple in marriage by the commitment they initially make and by the way they treat one another all the days of their life.

SOCIAL CONTRACT

The contractual side of marriage, therefore, involves not only husband and wife but also Almighty God himself and the community of which the couple is a part. That is why Jesus said: "Man must not separate, then, what God has joined together" (Matthew 19:6). Consequently, because God joins people in rightful marriage, the responsibilities of marriage are not those only which you may choose to agree on between yourselves.

Various responsibilities are established by God himself in the Scripture. These responsibilities derive from the mutual help you are to give one another, the self-sacrificing love you share, and your unity, which is closer than any other human relationship. To encourage, help, and, in a sense, monitor the marital relationship, the community shares not only in the wedding but also in what follows throughout the marriage. To accomplish these purposes, customs of the community (from family on out) may be more significant than law.

In a sense marriage is also a social contract in which the terms of the relationship are set in part by the community. Though these terms are never as primary as those set by God's revelation and seldom as specific as those the couple may devise, they nevertheless must be taken into account. To defy them is to run into considerable peril.

In the letter of Paul to the Ephesians there is a verse at the end of Chapter 4 which can well be a pattern for any marriage. Paul addresses it to all who follow Christ, but it fits beautifully for the marriage relationship. He says, "Be generous to one another, tenderhearted, forgiving one another as God in Christ forgave you."

Many a mother has said to her son-in-law as he and his bride took off for their new home, "Be good to her." In that simple plea is a world of marital wisdom. If only both husband and wife will freely accept that responsibility and seek to fulfill it always, things will go well. But they must be good to one another in ways that the recipient—and not just the bestower—understands and appreciates. Furthermore, to be good to one another in marriage in the full sense, the good must be free and open, not as though one were ashamed of it or doing it as a great concession.

Husbands particularly are not always generous to their wives. If they are, it is one of the really appreciated actions for which their wives will be proud of them and will love them. If that generosity extends not only to money and time but also to sincere praise for the wife, the bond is thereby more firmly knit. But wives, too, need to be generous to their husbands so that their pleasant words and merry hours are not only those they give to others but those which they give especially to their husbands. As they give themselves, their time, their effort, and especially, their interest first of all to their husbands, their generosity wakens a positive response.

To be good to one another in intention and action, openly and freely, makes for a wholesome relationship in marriage. Between husband and wife, more easily than in any other relationship, it should be possible to follow the Apostle's exhortation to be "tender-hearted."

VULNERABILITY

Husband and wife are admittedly vulnerable to one another. It takes no great skill for a husband or wife to devise ways to wound one another. But it does take great effort all the years of marriage to nurture a continuing relationship of tenderness. Especially when things go reasonably well and each becomes successful in his or her own interests, it is easy to take one another for granted. When this begins to happen, the change may be so gradual as to first be unnoticed or, at least, difficult to complain about. But sooner or later one or both will realize that the former expressions of regard, interest, and affection no longer occur.

If husband and wife will seek to be good to one another, tenderly, then the all-important element the Apostle adds will be easier, too: "forgive one another as God in Christ forgives you." For the time comes when human frailty and circumstances combine to make husband and wife thoughtless, unjust, unkind, or irresponsible toward one another. If you can together approach the throne of God and remember his unlimited mercy in Jesus Christ and then feel confident in one another's basic good will, you will forgive.

It is, after all, in sturdy Christian faith, dependent on God's mercy through Jesus, that all of life is to be lived. Showing, as best one can, the goodness and power of God, so that how we deal with people stems from that root, enriches all human life.

UNSELFISH LOVE

The unrestrained joy of a wedding derives, in part, from the promise and hope such an entirely new start in life implies for the bridal couple. But perhaps there is more. It may be that a wedding asserts in a unique way the human capacity for unselfish love and for free choice. It reflects the exuberance such love and free choice brings. It is a time to promise to be good to one another always and to learn to do so openly.

It is not possible to recommend too highly the relationship of marriage which bears so clearly the mark of God's plan for most human lives. Marriage gives human beings an opportunity for secure love and an experience of sharing that can discipline them in wholesome ways. Though, of course, in seeking a mate you cannot be totally unselfish, that is, you must consider what you desire and what brings benefit to you, once the marriage is entered upon, the emphasis must fall on what you can do for the other person.

There are few warmer, more delightful scenes in life than a man and woman who love one another and care for one another faithfully. Only if we add to that picture their common devotion to God and the willing sharing of their lives with children is the scene even more beautiful. Though there will always be hurts and deficiencies in a marital relationship because of human frailty, the joy, strength, and usefulness to others which family life affords makes it a blessing to many.

If you will love one another unselfishly, honor God faithfully, and serve others together as you do your duty in the various responsibilities of life, your marriage, too, will bring joy to you and blessing to others. A marriage involves our whole being, intellect, body, and emotions, and will require effort at every stage from the day of the wedding to the last anniversary, but it also offers great satisfaction. Without God's help no one can make marriage what it is intended to be. Even the opportunity for marriage is best received as a blessing from God.

Marriage is a gift of God, a common gift intended for most people, by which human beings find greater fulfillment and satisfaction than they can ordinarily achieve alone. But simply getting married does not automatically produce happiness.

A good marriage takes effort, understanding, patience, forgiveness, perseverance, and, above all, love. There will be tensions, not only now and then but all the time. It is the nature of human existence. But there is no need to panic. God's grace, care, and guidance can make marriage what God intends: a fulfillment of the human condition for meaning, joy, and purpose.

By the grace and blessing of God a husband and wife can make a good marriage that will be a joy to them and a blessing to others. Marriage is for two, in which each must do an equally important part, but it can create a unity which makes the two one throughout their days on earth.

THINGS TO CONSIDER

1. Discuss: "In the marriage relationship longsuffering martyrs—even willing martyrs—are seldom appreciated by their spouses."
2. What is meant by "a subordination of self-interest out of concern for the spouse"?
3. What is the nature of equality between male and female in marriage?
4. In what sense is marriage a contract?
5. What is meant by "marriage is not only a matter of the heart, but also of the head"?
6. How "unselfish" should you be in choosing a mate?
7. What does it mean to be "good to one another" in marriage?
8. Discuss "vulnerability" in marriage.